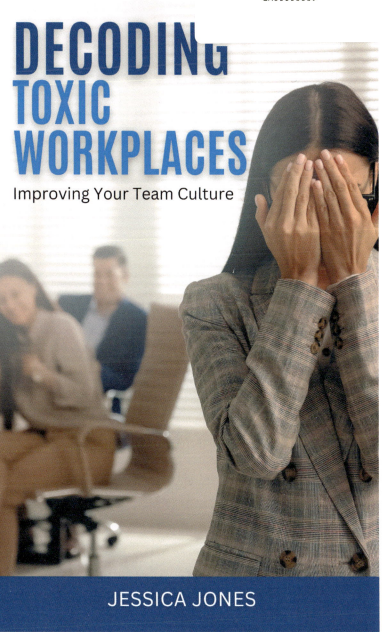

DECODING TOXIC WORKPLACES

Improving Your Team Culture

JESSICA JONES

Copyright © Jessica Jones 2024

All rights reserved. No part of this book, "Decoding Toxic Workplaces," may be reproduced, distributed, or transmitted in any form or by any means, including photocopying, recording, or other electronic or mechanical methods, without the prior written permission of the author, except in the case of brief quotations embodied in critical reviews and certain other noncommercial uses permitted by copyright law. For permission requests, contact the author through the website: www.thecodegroup.org.

Unauthorized use or reproduction of any part of this book is strictly prohibited and may result in legal action. Thank you for respecting the hard work of the author.

Decoding Toxic Workplaces 01

Thank you for purchasing my book. As the CEO of The CODE Group and author of this book, I am delighted to share insights on, "Decoding Toxic Workplaces: Improving Your Team Culture," with you. At The CODE Group, our mission is to empower organizations to unlock their full potential by fostering healthy, inclusive, and thriving workplace cultures.

For years, The CODE Group has worked with clients to eliminate internal threats like workplace toxicity, leveraging our expertise and insights to help organizations identify, address, and overcome harmful dynamics. Through our tailored consulting services and training programs, we are honored to help organizations build healthier, more vibrant workplaces.

As you embark on this journey, I encourage you to approach each chapter with an open mind and a spirit of curiosity. Reflect on how the concepts and strategies presented here resonate with your own experiences and challenges. Consider how you can apply these insights within your organization to drive positive change and foster a culture of trust, collaboration, and innovation.

Remember, the journey towards healthier workplaces is not a sprint but a marathon. It requires dedication, perseverance, and a willingness to challenge the status quo. But rest assured, you are not alone. The CODE Group is here to support you every step of the way, with guidance, training, and expertise to help you navigate the twists and turns of this transformative journey.

Together, let us rise to the challenge of creating workplaces where individuals thrive, and toxicity has no place to hide. Together, let's make going to work more enjoyable for everyone.

~ *Jessica Jones*

Jessica Jones
CEO, The CODE Group

Table of Contents

Introduction	03
Section 1: Recognizing the Signs of Toxicity	05
Section 2: Underlying Causes of Toxicity	16
Section 3: Strategies for Resolution and Prevention	33
Conclusion	47

Introduction

In the vast landscape of modern workplaces, there exists a silent but formidable adversary: **toxicity**. It lurks within the halls of even the most esteemed organizations, sowing seeds of discontent, demoralization, and dysfunction. When toxicity is present, productivity dwindles, creativity withers, and employees suffer in silence. That is the reality of toxic workplaces.

Understanding the Impact of Toxic Workplaces

Before we begin to decode the intricacies of toxic workplaces, let us first grasp their profound impact. Imagine a workspace with no camaraderie, only relentless competition and distrust. Picture employees, who were once enthusiastic and engaged, now worn down by the relentless onslaught of negativity and discouragement. Such environments impair individual well-being and sabotage collective progress, stifling innovation and eroding organizational cohesion.

The toll of toxic workplaces extends far beyond the confines of office walls. Mental health suffers, absenteeism rises, and turnover rates skyrocket as individuals seek refuge from the toxic disorder. The results of toxicity are felt throughout society, as disillusioned employees carry their grievances home, affecting relationships, communities, and broader societal structures.

Why Addressing Toxicity is Essential for Organizational Health

In the face of such dire consequences, addressing workplace toxicity emerges not merely as an option but as an imperative for organizational health and longevity. Much like a festering wound, toxicity infects everyone and everything around it. If left unchecked, it spreads like cancer, destroying the foundation of individual and organizational success.

It is extremely dangerous for organizations to turn a blind eye to toxicity. Beyond the human cost, toxicity takes a heavy toll on the bottom line, eroding profitability, tarnishing reputations, and hindering growth. In today's hyper-connected world, where information spreads quickly, the repercussions of a toxic workplace can be swift and unforgiving, leading to irreparable damage to your brand and your customers' or investors' confidence.

Overview of Toxic Workplace Dynamics

To confront the plague of toxicity head-on, we must first understand its complex nature. Toxic workplaces are not impenetrable entities but rather intricate environments shaped by a multitude of negative factors. From toxic leadership behaviors and dysfunctional power dynamics to ingrained cultural norms and unchecked psychological pressures, the roots of toxicity run deep.

In the coming chapters, we will delve into the unique aspects of toxic workplace dynamics, illuminating the hidden forces that perpetuate toxicity while exploring strategies to dismantle them. Through case studies, expert insights, and actionable advice, I will equip you with the tools and knowledge to identify, address, and overcome toxic workplace dynamics.

As we embark on this journey together, let's approach these concepts introspectively and with intentional foresight for future actions. Let's cultivate workplaces where trust flourishes, collaboration thrives, and individuals can unleash their full potential.

Section 1: Recognizing Toxicity in the Workplace

- Chapter 1: Identifying Common Toxic Behaviors and Attitudes
- Chapter 2: Assessing the Impact on Employees and the Organization
- Chapter 3: Toxicity Case Studies

CHAPTER 1: IDENTIFYING COMMON TOXIC BEHAVIORS AND ATTITUDES

In the murky waters of a toxic workplace, recognizing the signs of trouble is the first step towards reclaiming clarity and restoring balance. In this section, we will embark on a journey of discovery, shining a light on the common behaviors, attitudes, and impacts that characterize toxic workplaces.

To combat toxicity effectively, one must first learn to recognize its insidious manifestations. From subtle microaggressions to overt displays of aggression, toxic behaviors and attitudes can take many forms. In this chapter, we will delve into some examples of toxicity, uncovering the telltale signs that betray its presence.

Gaslighting: The Art of Psychological Manipulation

Gaslighting is a term that comes from the 1944 film "Gaslight." It refers to the deliberate manipulation of someone into questioning their own sanity. In toxic workplaces, gaslighting is a potent weapon used by a colleague or superior to manipulate or distort facts, events, or conversations in order to undermine a coworker's perceptions. This can cause the coworker to doubt their own sanity or judgment.

Undermining: The Silent Saboteur
Undermining behaviors erode trust and breed dysfunction within teams, sabotaging productivity and morale. Whether through backstabbing or withholding vital information, underminers sow seeds of discord, fueling a toxic atmosphere of suspicion and resentment.

Perfectionism: The Double-Edged Sword
While a commitment to excellence is commendable, toxic perfectionism crosses the line into harmful territory. In environments where perfection is not just valued but demanded at all costs, employees are subjected to unrelenting pressure, leading to burnout, anxiety, and diminished well-being.

Micromanagement: The Suffocating Supervisor
Micromanagement occurs when a manager attempts to control and monitor every aspect of their employees' work. This often leads to decreased autonomy, demotivation, and a lack of trust. Micromanagement stifles creativity, impedes productivity, and fosters a culture of fear and frustration.

Lack of Accountability: The Blame Game
In toxic environments, individuals may avoid taking responsibility for their actions or outcomes, shifting blame onto others or making excuses. Lack of accountability erodes trust within teams, creates resentment, and hinders problem-solving and collaboration, ultimately undermining transparency and integrity within the organization.

Gossip and Rumor-Mongering: The Toxic Grapevine
Toxic workplaces often foster an environment where gossip and rumor-mongering thrive. This behavior involves spreading hearsay, misinformation, or malicious rumors about colleagues, creating a culture of distrust, insecurity, and negativity. Gossip damages professional relationships, harms reputations, and distracts from productive work.

25 Behaviors and Attitudes that Foster Toxicity at Work

1. Lack of trust among team members and leadership.
2. Constant gossiping and spreading of rumors.
3. Micromanagement and a lack of autonomy.
4. Bullying, harassment, or intimidation.
5. Favoritism and nepotism in decision-making.
6. High levels of stress and burnout among employees.
7. Lack of clear communication and transparency.
8. Blaming and finger-pointing when things go wrong.
9. Poor work-life balance and excessive workload.
10. Lack of recognition and appreciation for employees' contributions.
11. Undermining and sabotaging colleagues' efforts.
12. Cliques or exclusionary behavior within the team.
13. Frequent conflicts and unresolved disputes.
14. Discrimination based on gender, race, age, or other factors.
15. Resistance to change and innovation.
16. Lack of accountability for actions and decisions.
17. Inconsistent enforcement of policies and procedures.
18. Low morale and disengagement among employees.
19. Fear of retaliation for speaking up or raising concerns.
20. Toxic leadership behaviors, such as arrogance or lack of concern / empathy.
21. Passive-aggressive communication and behavior.
22. Overemphasis on competition rather than collaboration.
23. Unrealistic expectations and goals set by leadership.
24. Lack of opportunities for career advancement or professional growth.
25. High turnover rates and difficulty retaining top talent.

CHAPTER 2: ASSESSING THE IMPACT ON EMPLOYEES AND THE ORGANIZATION

Toxicity within organizations is not just a matter of inconvenience or discomfort; it has profound and far-reaching consequences that affect both individuals and the organization's collective culture. In this chapter, we will explore the multifaceted impact of toxic workplaces on employees' mental health and well-being and the broader implications for organizational productivity and performance.

The Human Cost: Mental Health and Well-Being

The toll that toxic workplaces take on employees' mental health and well-being cannot be overstated. Chronic exposure to toxic behaviors can lead to a range of psychological and emotional challenges, ultimately affecting individuals both inside and outside of work.

1. **Stress and Anxiety:** Employees in toxic environments often experience heightened levels of stress and anxiety. The constant fear of conflict, unpredictability, and negative repercussions can create a persistent state of tension, making it difficult for individuals to feel at ease in their work environment.

2. **Depression and Burnout**: Prolonged exposure to toxic dynamics can contribute to feelings of depression and eventual burnout. Employees may struggle with hopelessness or helplessness, feeling trapped in an environment that undermines their sense of worth and purpose.

3. **Impaired Relationships and Isolation**: Toxic cultures erode trust and collaboration, leading to strained relationships and social isolation among team members. Individuals may withdraw or become defensive as they navigate an atmosphere of negativity and distrust.

Coping Strategies and Support: Organizations must prioritize mental health support and provide resources to help employees cope and build personal resilience.
- Encourage open communication and normalize discussions around mental health.
- Motivate employees to support each other by offering encouragement, assistance, and fostering connections as appropriate.
- Offer access to counseling services, employee assistance programs (EAPs), and mental health resources.
- Promote work-life balance and self-care practices to help employees manage stress and maintain well-being.

The Organizational Toll: Productivity and Performance

The detrimental impact of toxicity extends beyond individual well-being to affect the overall productivity and performance of the organization. Toxic environments breed inefficiency, hindering progress and innovation.

1. **Distraction and Disengagement**: Employees in toxic workplaces may find themselves preoccupied with navigating interpersonal conflicts or managing emotional stress, diverting their attention from core job responsibilities. Being distracted or disengaged leads to decreased focus and engagement.

2. **High Turnover and Recruitment Costs**: Toxic cultures drive talented employees away, resulting in high turnover rates and increased recruitment costs. Constantly replacing team members disrupts workflow and diminishes institutional knowledge.

3. **Diminished Creativity and Innovation**: Toxic environments stifle ideas, creativity, and innovation. Fear of failure or reprisal discourages risk-taking and experimentation, limiting the organization's ability to adapt and thrive in a competitive landscape.

Strategies for Mitigation and Improvement: Organizations must take proactive measures to address and reduce toxic behaviors in the wor toxic.
- Foster a culture of trust, transparency, and accountability through clear communication and ethical leadership.
- Implement robust conflict resolution processes and invest in training for managers to effectively recognize and address toxic behaviors.
- Promote inclusivity and belonging to create a supportive and respectful work environment where all employees feel valued and em to creat

In conclusion, understanding the impact of toxicity on both individuals and the organization is critical for leaders and organizations committed to cultivating a healthy and thriving team culture. By prioritizing mental health support, fostering a positive work environment, and addressing toxic behaviors head-on, organizations can pave the way for sustained productivity, innovation, and employee well-being.

CHAPTER THREE: TOXICITY CASE STUDIES

Throughout history, cautionary tales of toxicity have existed in many forms. The following case studies serve as poignant reminders of the subtle nature of toxicity and the havoc it wreaks on individuals, teams, and entire organizations. Through these examples, we gain invaluable insights into the diverse manifestations of toxicity and its profound impact on organizational health and well-being.

Case Study 1: Micromanagement
In Company X, a once-promising startup known for its innovative products, a culture of micromanagement took root. Every aspect of employees' work was scrutinized and controlled, stifling creativity and autonomy. Managers hovered over employees' shoulders, dictating every detail of their tasks and processes. Despite initial success, morale plummeted, turnover rates soared, and innovation ground to a halt. Ultimately, Company X became a cautionary tale of how micromanagement can strangle an organization's potential and drive away its most talented employees.

Key Takeaways:
This case study underscores the corrosive effects of micromanagement on employee morale, autonomy, and innovation. It serves as a stark reminder that trust is the lifeblood of any organization and that leaders must resist the temptation to exert excessive control over their teams.

Case Study 2: Office Politics

In Organization Y, a toxic culture of office politics poisoned the workplace environment. Employees jockeyed for favoritism, engaged in gossip and backstabbing behavior, and formed alliances to advance their personal agendas. Trust eroded, collaboration faltered, and productivity suffered as employees devoted more time and energy to navigating the political minefield than to fulfilling their job responsibilities. In the end, Organization Y found itself mired in dysfunction, needing assistance to harness its workforce's collective talents for the greater good.

Key Takeaways:

This case study highlights the destructive power of office politics and its detrimental impact on organizational culture and performance. It underscores the importance of fostering a culture of transparency, fairness, and merit-based advancements, where individuals are judged based on their contributions rather than their political savvy.

Case Study 3: Toxic Leadership

In Company Z, a charismatic but tyrannical CEO ruled with an iron fist, instilling fear and intimidation in his employees. Dissent was silenced, innovation was stifled, and employees constantly feared retaliation. Despite the outward appearance of success, morale was at an all-time low, and turnover rates were alarmingly high. Eventually, the toxic leadership culture caught up with Company Z, leading to a mass exodus of talent and a tarnished reputation from which it struggled to recover.

Key Takeaways:

This case study is a stark reminder of leadership's pivotal role in shaping organizational culture and dynamics. It underscores the importance of cultivating emotionally intelligent leaders who lead with empathy, humility, and integrity rather than resorting to fear and intimidation.

As we reflect on these case studies, let us heed the lessons they imparted and commit to building workplaces where toxicity has no place to thrive. Through awareness, empathy, and proactive intervention, we can create environments where individuals feel valued, empowered, and inspired to do their best work.

Self-Reflective Questions for Section 1: Recognizing Toxicity in the Workplace

Take a quick pause to reflect on the following questions to help you evaluate your experiences and perceptions of toxicity in your workplace:

- **Am I often made to feel insecure or inadequate in my work?**
    - *When have I felt undermined, belittled, or devalued by colleagues or superiors? How did these experiences impact my confidence and performance?*

- **Do I experience frequent interactions that I would characterize as micromanagement or lack of trust?**
    - *Am I the subject of excessive monitoring? Does my manager try to control my tasks? Is trust and autonomy lacking in my work relationships? How do these dynamics affect my motivation and job satisfaction?*

- **Have I witnessed or been subjected to patterns of blame-shifting or excuse-making?**
    - *Do my colleagues or superiors avoid accountability for their actions or deflect blame onto others? How does this behavior impact team dynamics and the overall work environment?*

- **Do I notice a culture of gossip, rumors, or negative talk among colleagues?**
    - *How prevalent is gossip and negative chatter within my workplace? How does participating in or being exposed to such conversations affect my morale, trust, and relationships with coworkers?*

- **How do I feel about my workplace's overall atmosphere and culture?**
    - *What is the general vibe and culture of my workplace? Does the culture foster collaboration, respect, and support, or is it characterized by tension, toxicity, and dysfunction? How does this atmosphere impact my well-being and professional growth?*

Section 2: Underlying Causes of Toxicity

- Chapter 4: Exploring Leadership Failures and Organizational Structures
- Chapter 5: Cultural Influences on Workplace Toxicity
- Chapter 6: Psychological Factors Contributing to Toxic Environments

Decoding Toxic Workplaces   17

Decoding toxic workplaces must go beyond surface-level observations and investigate the underlying factors that cause toxicity. In this section, we will explore the intricate interplay of leadership failures, organizational structures, cultural influences, and psychological factors that fuel the flames of toxicity within organizations.

CHAPTER 4: EXPLORING LEADERSHIP FAILURES AND ORGANIZATIONAL STRUCTURES

Leadership is the compass that guides an organization's journey, shaping its culture, values, and priorities. Yet, when leadership falters, the consequences can be dire. This chapter examines how leadership failures contribute to toxicity within organizations. From authoritarian leadership styles that breed fear and resentment to laissez-faire approaches that foster chaos and uncertainty, the impact of leadership on organizational health cannot be overstated.

We understand that how an organization is structured can either help or hinder the development of a positive work environment. Hierarchical structures with strict rules and decisions made only by top-level leaders can stifle innovation and discourage open communication, creating an environment where toxicity can thrive. On the other hand, flat organizational structures that prioritize collaboration, autonomy, and transparency can build a culture of trust and empowerment, reducing the risk of toxicity.

Additionally, we will explore the root causes of leadership failures and organizational dysfunctions to equip you with the knowledge and tools needed to identify and address these issues within your organizations.

20 Leadership Failures that Contribute to a Toxic Work Environment

1. Lack of clear communication and transparency.
2. Micromanagement and a lack of trust in employees' abilities.
3. Failure to address conflicts or disputes within the team.
4. Favoritism and unfair treatment of certain employees.
5. Failure to provide adequate support or resources for employees.
6. Ignoring or dismissing employees' concerns and feedback.
7. Setting unrealistic expectations or goals without providing necessary guidance or support.
8. Lack of accountability for leaders' actions or decisions.
9. Creating a culture of fear or intimidation through harsh communication or disciplinary measures.
10. Failure to recognize or reward employees' contributions and achievements.
11. Lack of empathy or understanding towards employees' personal or professional challenges.
12. Inconsistency in enforcing policies and procedures.
13. Failure to address issues of harassment or discrimination in the workplace.
14. Failure to promote diversity, equity, inclusion, and accessibility (DEIA) within the organization.
15. Allowing toxic behaviors, such as gossiping or undermining, to go unchecked.
16. Making decisions based on personal biases or preferences rather than objective criteria.
17. Failure to provide opportunities for professional development and growth.
18. Ignoring or downplaying the importance of work-life balance for employees.
19. Failure to lead by example and uphold ethical standards of conduct.
20. Lack of vision or direction, resulting in employees' confusion and uncertainty.

These leadership failures can contribute to a toxic work environment by eroding trust, creating resentment, and fostering a culture of dysfunction within a team. Addressing these issues requires leaders to commit to listening to employees' concerns, taking responsibility for their actions, and actively working towards creating a healthier and more supportive workplace.

Understanding the Root Causes of Leadership Failures and Organizational Dysfunctions

Understanding the various forms of leadership failures and how they can manifest as organizational dysfunction conveys the far-reaching consequences for employee morale, productivity, and overall organizational health. To effectively address these issues, it is essential to understand the root causes that contribute to their emergence. By equipping ourselves with this knowledge, we can empower organizations to identify and address these issues within their environments.

Lack of Vision and Direction:
Leadership failures often stem from a need for a clearer vision and direction for the organization. When leaders fail to articulate a compelling vision or set strategic goals, employees can feel adrift and uncertain about the organization's purpose and priorities. This lack of clarity can lead to disengagement, inefficiency, and a lack of alignment among team members.

Poor Communication and Transparency:
Effective communication is the lifeblood of any organization, yet leadership failures often arise from a need for transparency and open communication channels. When leaders fail to communicate openly and honestly with their team, it can breed mistrust, rumors, and speculation. Moreover, poor communication leads to misunderstandings, misalignment of goals, and a breakdown in collaboration and teamwork.

Failure to Foster a Culture of Trust and Accountability:
Leadership failures can also result from a failure to foster a culture of trust and accountability within an organization.

When leaders fail to lead by example and hold themselves and others accountable for their actions, trust erodes, and morale declines. Moreover, a lack of accountability can lead to a culture of blame-shifting, finger-pointing, and avoidance of responsibility, hindering the organization's ability to learn and grow from its mistakes.

Ineffective Decision-Making Processes:
Organizational dysfunctions often arise from ineffective decision-making processes, where decisions are made impulsively without sufficient input or consideration of potential consequences. When leaders fail to solicit diverse perspectives, weigh alternative options, or consider the long-term implications of their decisions, it can lead to poor outcomes, employee resistance, and a lack of buy-in from stakeholders.

Resistance to Change and Innovation:
Leadership failures can also stem from resistance to change and innovation within the organization. When leaders cling to outdated practices, resist new ideas, or fail to adapt to changing market conditions or trends, it stifles creativity, innovation, and growth. A lack of openness to change can lead to complacency, stagnation, and irrelevance in today's fast-paced business environment.

Empowering You to Drive Positive Change:
Understanding the root causes of leadership failures and organizational dysfunctions is crucial for taking proactive steps to address these issues within your own organization. This may involve creating a culture of open communication and transparency, setting clear expectations and goals, promoting accountability at all levels, and embracing change and innovation as opportunities for growth and improvement. With the knowledge and tools needed to identify and address these issues, we create healthier and more resilient organizations that are better equipped to navigate the challenges of today's constantly changing business landscape.

CHAPTER 5: CULTURAL INFLUENCES ON WORKPLACE TOXICITY

Culture shapes an organization's values, norms, and behaviors. Yet, when culture becomes toxic, it can poison the roots of organizational health and vitality. In this chapter, we will explore the cultural influences that contribute to workplace toxicity, from toxic masculinity and power dynamics to the normalization of toxic behaviors such as overwork and burnout.

We will delve into the role of organizational rituals, symbols, and language in perpetuating toxic cultures, shedding light on how seemingly innocuous practices can reinforce harmful norms and attitudes. Moreover, we will examine the impact of diversity, equity, inclusion, and accessibility (DEIA) initiatives on organizational culture, exploring how efforts to promote equity and combat discrimination can mitigate the risk of toxicity and foster a culture of belonging and respect.

Through thought-provoking insights and practical strategies, I want to empower you to challenge entrenched cultural norms and champion positive change within your teams, creating environments where all individuals feel valued, respected, and empowered to succeed.

Culture is the invisible force that drives the very essence of an organization. It encompasses the values, beliefs, and behaviors that guide interactions among individuals and define the organization's brand and reputation. However, when culture becomes toxic, it seeps into every aspect of organizational life, poisoning relationships, decreasing innovative ideas, and breaking down trust. Examining the cultural influences that contribute to workplace toxicity, from the dangerous effects of toxic masculinity and power dynamics to the normalization of harmful behaviors like overwork and burnout, let's examine the hidden forces that perpetuate toxicity in organizational cultures. By analyzing ourselves and our workplace cultures and applying practical strategies, we challenge toxic cultural norms and cultivate environments where all individuals can thrive.

Toxic Masculinity and Power Dynamics

Toxic masculinity refers to the adherence to traditional masculine norms that promote aggression, dominance, and emotional suppression. In many workplaces, these toxic norms perpetuate power imbalances and reinforce harmful behaviors such as sexism, harassment, and discrimination. By examining the ways in which toxic masculinity and power dynamics intersect within organizational cultures, we can begin to understand how these dynamics contribute to workplace toxicity and perpetuate inequalities.

Five examples of how toxic masculinity can manifest in the workplace, contributing to a hostile or unproductive environment include:
- **Dominance and Aggression**: Toxic masculinity may lead to a culture where dominance and aggression are glorified or expected, often resulting in confrontational interactions, bullying, or intimidation tactics.
- **Dismissal of emotions and vulnerability:** Toxic masculinity norms often discourage men from expressing emotions or showing vulnerability. This can lead to a lack of empathy and emotional support, resulting in the projection of this behavior towards others, especially women.

- **Sexual Harassment and Misconduct**: Toxic masculinity may contribute to a culture where sexual harassment and misconduct are normalized or excused. This can involve inappropriate comments, advances, or actions towards coworkers, creating a hostile and unsafe work environment.
- **Rigid Gender Stereotypes**: Toxic masculinity perpetuates rigid gender stereotypes that prescribe specific traits and behaviors to men, such as aggressiveness, indifference, and competitiveness. This can marginalize individuals who do not conform to these norms, leading to discrimination, exclusion, or microaggressions in the workplace.
- **Resistance to Diversity and Inclusion Efforts**: Toxic masculinity may lead to resistance towards diversity and inclusion efforts aimed at promoting gender equality and challenging traditional gender roles. This resistance can manifest through skepticism towards initiatives promoting gender diversity, discriminatory hiring practices, or backlash against inclusive policies.

Addressing toxic masculinity in the workplace requires a commitment to challenging harmful gender norms, promoting respect and empathy, and creating an inclusive environment. Through exercises and discussions, your team will gain insight into cultural influences in your organization to challenge toxic masculinity and power structures.

Normalization of Toxic Behaviors

In today's hyper-competitive work environment, the pressure to perform at all costs has led to the normalization of toxic behaviors such as overwork, burnout, and workaholism. These behaviors harm individuals' well-being and perpetuate a culture of toxicity within organizations.

Explore the root causes of these toxic behaviors and their impact on your organizational culture to better understand how seemingly harmless practices can contribute to workplace toxicity.

Challenging the normalization of toxic behaviors like overwork, burnout, and workaholism requires a concerted effort to promote a healthier work-life balance and prioritize employee well-being. Below are three effective strategies:

1. **Promote Work-Life Balance Initiatives:**
   - Implement policies and programs prioritizing work-life balance, such as flexible work hours, remote work options, and paid time off. Encourage employees to take breaks, utilize vacation time, and disconnect from work outside of business hours.
   - Lead by example and model healthy work habits and boundaries. Encourage managers and team leaders to support work-life balance initiatives and respect employees' personal time.

2. **Foster a Culture of Open Communication and Support:**
   - Create a supportive work environment where employees feel comfortable openly discussing their workload, stress levels, and personal challenges without fear of judgment or reprisal.
   - Offer resources and support for stress management, mental health, and well-being, such as Employee Assistance Programs (EAPs), counseling services, or workshops on resilience and mindfulness.

3. **Set Realistic Expectations and Boundaries:**
   - Encourage realistic goal-setting and prioritize tasks based on importance and urgency to prevent overwork and burnout. Provide adequate resources and support to help employees manage their workload effectively.
   - Establish clear boundaries around work hours, email expectations, and after-hours communication. Encourage employees to unplug and recharge outside of work hours.

By implementing these strategies, organizations can challenge the normalization of toxic behaviors like overwork, burnout, and workaholism and create a culture prioritizing employee well-being and sustainable productivity.

Diversity, Equity, Inclusion and Accessibility Initiatives

Diversity, equity, inclusion and accessibility (DEIA) initiatives play a crucial role in shaping organizational culture and mitigating the risk of toxicity. By promoting diversity of thought, experience, and background, organizations can foster a culture of belonging and respect where all individuals feel valued and empowered to succeed. By simply acknowledging and implementing effective DEIA initiatives like training, employee resource groups, corporate branding and messaging, and gender equity in task distribution, we cultivate cultures of belonging and respect within our own organizations.

DEIA initiatives help diminish toxicity by:
1. Promoting understanding and empathy to recognize and value diverse perspectives, experiences, and identities.
2. Enhances collaboration and innovation by creating an environment where all voices are heard and valued.
3. Increases employee engagement and satisfaction by fostering a sense of belonging and respect.
4. Reduces bias and discrimination in hiring, promotion, and decision-making processes.
5. Strengthens organizational reputation and competitiveness to attract top talent and enhance their competitive advantage in the marketplace.

As we conclude our exploration of how culture affects workplace toxicity, it's important to remember the profound impact an organization's culture has on the well-being and success of individuals and the entire team. By understanding the underlying causes of toxic cultural norms and behaviors, we can confront them with courage and conviction, fostering environments where everyone feels they belong and are empowered to succeed, and toxicity cannot thrive.

CHAPTER 6: PSYCHOLOGICAL FACTORS CONTRIBUTING TO TOXIC ENVIRONMENTS

At the heart of every toxic workplace lies a complex web of psychological factors that shape individual attitudes, behaviors, and interactions. In this chapter, we explore the psychological underpinnings of toxicity, from cognitive biases and personality traits to the role of stress, trauma, and mental health issues in perpetuating toxic dynamics.

As we explore the concept of psychological safety and its crucial role in creating a positive work environment, it's important to give individuals the freedom to voice their opinions, take risks, and be themselves without fear of judgment or retaliation. Additionally, we must analyze the concept of groupthink and its influence on decision-making in organizations, investigating how the desire for conformity and consensus can hinder creativity and dissent.

Through illuminating case studies and expert insights, we can understand the hidden psychological forces that drive toxic behaviors and attitudes within organizations. By increasing awareness of these factors and offering strategies to mitigate their impact, we will create workplaces where psychological well-being is prioritized and toxicity is not tolerated.

Cognitive Biases and Personality Traits:
Humans are inherently prone to cognitive biases — mental shortcuts that distort our perception of reality and influence our decision-making processes. From confirmation bias, which leads us to seek information that confirms our preconceived beliefs, to the halo effect, which causes us to form overall impressions of people based on specific traits, cognitive biases shape how we interpret and respond to the world around us. Individual personality traits, such as narcissism, Machiavellianism, and psychopathy, can exacerbate toxic behaviors and attitudes within the workplace, creating environments characterized by manipulation, exploitation, and disregard for others' well-being.

The Role of Stress, Trauma, and Mental Health:

The pressures of modern work life - intense competition, long hours, and relentless performance expectations - can affect employees' mental health and well-being. Chronic stress, unresolved trauma, and untreated mental health issues can fuel toxic behaviors such as aggression, hostility, workplace violence, and emotional volatility. Moreover, the stigma surrounding mental health in many workplaces can exacerbate feelings of shame and isolation, preventing individuals from seeking the support they need and perpetuating a culture of silence and suffering.

Chronic mild stress, characterized by persistent, low-level stressors and daily challenges, is pervasive in today's workplaces, affecting a significant portion of the workforce. According to the American Institute of Stress, approximately 83% of workers experience stress related to their jobs, with 25% reporting it as the leading cause of their stress. While these stressors may appear minor individually, their cumulative impact can be substantial, contributing to decreased productivity, morale, and overall well-being.

Employees grappling with chronic mild stress often exhibit symptoms such as irritability, fatigue, and diminished motivation, hindering their ability to perform optimally and collaborate effectively with colleagues. Prolonged exposure to stressors can heighten tension, conflict, and negativity within teams, fostering a toxic work environment characterized by burnout, cynicism, and disengagement. As organizations strive to address the prevalence of chronic mild stress, it becomes increasingly imperative to implement strategies that promote employee well-being, resilience, and a positive workplace culture.

Psychological Safety:

The concept of psychological safety is central to fostering a healthy work environment - the belief that one can speak up, take risks, and express oneself without fear of negative consequences. In psychologically safe workplaces, individuals feel empowered to share their ideas, voice their concerns, and challenge the status quo. By creating an atmosphere of trust, respect, and open communication, you can nurture psychological safety and cultivate cultures where diverse perspectives are valued and innovation thrives.

Five tips to encourage psychological safety at work include:
1. Model vulnerability, openness, and admitting mistakes, demonstrating that it is safe to speak up and take risks.
2. Hold regular team meetings, brainstorming sessions, or check-ins where everyone is encouraged to participate and contribute.
3. Encourage respectful and constructive feedback across the team, focusing on behaviors and actions rather than personal characteristics.
4. Encourage collaboration and teamwork, emphasizing the importance of supporting one another and working towards common goals.
5. Provide conflict resolution training and encourage open dialogue to address issues before they escalate.

Groupthink and Decision-Making Processes:
Groupthink — the tendency for group members to seek consensus and avoid conflict at all costs, even at the expense of critical thinking and independent judgment — can undermine psychological safety. In environments characterized by groupthink, dissenting voices are silenced, alternative viewpoints are dismissed, and flawed decisions are made without proper scrutiny. Organizations can mitigate the risk of faulty decision-making processes and foster a culture of critical thinking and innovation by understanding the dangers of groupthink and promoting a culture of constructive dissent and debate.

The following case studies uncover the hidden psychological forces that drive toxic behaviors and attitudes within organizations.

Case Study 1: The Impact of Narcissistic Leadership:
In a large marketing agency, the CEO, John, was known for his charismatic personality and grandiose vision for the company. However, behind the facade of success lay a toxic leadership style driven by narcissistic tendencies. John routinely dismissed the input of his employees, taking credit for their ideas and blaming them for any failures. He created a culture of fear and intimidation, where employees felt powerless to speak up or challenge his decisions. As a result, morale plummeted, turnover rates soared, and productivity suffered.

Psychological Insight: Narcissistic leaders often prioritize their own ego and image over the well-being of their employees, creating toxic environments characterized by manipulation, exploitation, and disregard for others' feelings. The fear of retaliation and the desire for approval from the narcissistic leader can lead employees to suppress their own opinions and conform to the leader's wishes, perpetuating a culture of toxicity and dysfunction.

Case Study 2: The Perils of Groupthink
In a technology startup, the leadership team was tasked with making a critical decision about the direction of a new product launch. Despite initial concerns from several team members about potential risks, the prevailing sentiment was to move forward with the launch without conducting thorough market research or feasibility studies. The group was dominated by a charismatic and persuasive leader who discouraged dissenting opinions and promoted a culture of conformity.

Psychological Insight: In environments characterized by groupthink, dissenting voices are suppressed, alternative viewpoints are ignored, and flawed decisions are made without proper risk and consequence evaluation. The fear of social rejection and the desire for group cohesion can lead individuals to conform to the prevailing group opinion, even if they harbor reservations or doubts.

Case Study 3: The Impact of Chronic Mild Stress on Workplace Toxicity

In a bustling corporate office, employees are constantly confronted with the relentless pressure of tight deadlines, demanding clients, and ever-increasing workloads. These stressors, though individually manageable, have cumulatively created an environment of chronic mild stress — a persistent state of tension and anxiety that has permeated the workplace.

As the pressure mounted, employees found themselves grappling with the relentless demands of their jobs. Fatigue, irritability, and feelings of overwhelm became the norm, leading to strained relationships, decreased productivity, and increased absenteeism. In this toxic environment, communication deteriorated, collaboration faltered, and trust disintegrated. Employees became increasingly isolated, focusing solely on surviving the day-to-day challenges rather than working together towards common goals.

Psychological Insight: Chronic mild stress can have dangerous effects on workplace culture, undermining morale and fueling toxic behaviors such as aggression, hostility, and emotional volatility. As individuals grapple with continuous stress, their cognitive resources become depleted, making it difficult to regulate their emotions and behavior effectively. This type of behavior can result in a witting or unwitting insider threat to an organization, who may cause harm to the security of the organization's information, people, or reputation.

Moreover, the pervasive nature of chronic mild stress can lead individuals to adopt maladaptive coping mechanisms, such as avoidance, withdrawal, or substance abuse, further exacerbating workplace toxicity. Without intervention, the cycle of stress and dysfunction continues, perpetuating a culture of negativity and discontent within the organization.

Self-Reflective Questions for Section 2: Underlying Causes of Toxicity

Let's take another quick pause to reflect on the following questions to help you evaluate the underlying causes of toxicity in your workplace:

- **How is conflict handled within my organization?**
    - *How is conflict managed and resolved in my workplace? Are there recurring patterns of avoidance, hostility, or ineffective communication?*

- **How does our organizational structure and leadership impact team dynamics?**
    - *What influences do organizational structure and leadership style have on our team's dynamics and workplace culture? Is micromanagement or lack of accountability present within my organization?*

- **What role does power dynamics play in shaping interactions and relationships?**
    - *What power dynamics are at play within my organization? Do power imbalances contribute to feelings of insecurity, resentment, or exploitation among our team?*

- **Are there cultural or normative factors that perpetuate toxic behaviors?**
    - *How do my team's values, beliefs, or norms regarding competition, success, or productivity contribute to a toxic work environment?*

- **How does my organization handle diversity, equity, inclusion, and accessibility (DEIA)?**
    - *What is my organization's approach to DEIA, and how does it impact workplace dynamics? Does my organization promote diversity, foster inclusivity, and address systemic biases to mitigate toxicity?*

Section 3: Strategies for Resolution and Prevention

- Chapter 7: Establishing a Culture of Transparency and Accountability
- Chapter 8: Implementing Effective Conflict Resolution Techniques
- Chapter 9: Building Trust and Empowerment Among Employees

In the battle against toxicity, knowledge is our most powerful weapon. Armed with insights gleaned from our exploration of toxic workplace dynamics and underlying causes, we are now ready to embark on the journey toward transformation. In this section, I aim to equip you with actionable strategies for addressing and overcoming toxicity within your organizations, fostering cultures of transparency, accountability, and trust.

CHAPTER 7: ESTABLISHING A CULTURE OF TRANSPARENCY AND ACCOUNTABILITY

Transparency is the cornerstone of trust, laying the foundation for open communication, collaboration, and accountability within organizations. In this chapter, we will explore practical strategies for fostering a culture of transparency, from promoting open-door policies and regular communication channels to providing employees with access to relevant information and decision-making processes.

Moreover, we will delve into the role of accountability in driving organizational performance and integrity, exploring strategies for holding individuals and teams accountable for their actions and outcomes. By promoting transparency and accountability at all levels of the organization, we can create environments where toxic behaviors are less likely to take root, and individuals feel empowered to speak up and take ownership of their work.

10 Practical Strategies to Foster a Culture of Transparency at Work

1. **Open-Door Policies**: Encourage leaders at all levels to adopt open-door policies, welcoming employees to approach them with questions, concerns, and feedback without fear. But don't put all of the responsibility on the employee; seek out conversations as a leader, too.
2. **Regular Communication Channels**: Establish regular communication channels, such as team meetings, newsletters, and town hall sessions, to inform employees about organizational updates, initiatives, and decisions.
3. **Transparent Goal Setting**: Involve employees in the goal-setting process, ensuring clarity and transparency around objectives, performance expectations, and individual roles in achieving them.
4. **Accessible Information**: Provide employees access to relevant information, resources, and data, enabling them to make informed decisions and understand the rationale behind organizational decisions.
5. **Clear Policies and Procedures**: Develop clear and concise policies and procedures for key organizational processes, such as hiring, promotion, and performance evaluation, ensuring transparency and consistency in decision-making.
6. **Feedback Mechanisms**: Implement formal feedback mechanisms, such as surveys, suggestion boxes, and anonymous hotlines, to solicit input and address concerns in a transparent manner.
7. **Transparency in Decision-Making**: Involve employees in decision-making processes, seeking their input and feedback on important initiatives, changes, and policies that affect them.
8. **Accountability and Follow-Up**: Hold leaders accountable for their actions and decisions, ensuring transparency and accountability in their interactions with employees and adherence to organizational values and policies.

10 Practical Strategies to Foster a Culture of Transparency at Work (continued)

9. **Training and Education**: Provide training and education on the importance of transparency in the workplace, highlighting the benefits of open communication, trust, and collaboration.
10. **Lead by Example**: Model transparent behavior and communication as a leader, demonstrating honesty, integrity, and openness in your interactions with employees and fostering a culture of transparency from the top down.

5 Strategies to Foster Accountability

1. **Establish Clear Expectations**: Clearly define roles, responsibilities, and performance expectations for individuals and teams. Ensure that everyone understands what is expected of them and how their contributions align with organizational goals and objectives.
2. **Set SMART Goals**: Utilize the SMART criteria (Specific, Measurable, Achievable, Relevant, Time-bound) when setting goals for individuals and teams. By making goals specific and measurable, it becomes easier to track progress and hold individuals accountable.
3. **Regular Check-Ins and Feedback**: Conduct regular check-ins to provide ongoing feedback to individuals and teams on their performance. Use these opportunities to discuss progress, address challenges, and provide support or resources as needed. You can help individuals stay on track and adjust as necessary by providing timely feedback.
4. **Implement Performance Metrics**: Establish key performance indicators (KPIs) and metrics to measure individual and team performance objectively. Monitor progress against these metrics regularly and provide feedback based on performance data. This allows individuals and teams to track their own progress and take ownership of their outcomes.
5. **Consequences and Rewards**: Establish consequences for failing to meet expectations and rewards for exceeding them. Make it clear that accountability is a two-way street, with both positive and negative consequences for actions and outcomes. By aligning consequences and rewards with performance, you reinforce the importance of accountability and motivate individuals and teams to strive for excellence.

By implementing these strategies, you can create a culture of accountability where individuals and teams take ownership of their actions and outcomes, driving performance and success.

CHAPTER 8: IMPLEMENTING EFFECTIVE CONFLICT RESOLUTION TECHNIQUES

Conflict is inevitable in our work life, arising from differences in perspectives, goals, and priorities. Yet, when left unaddressed, conflict can escalate into toxic dynamics that poison the well-being of individuals and teams. This chapter explores effective conflict resolution techniques for diffusing tensions, fostering understanding, and finding mutually beneficial solutions.

We will delve into the importance of active listening, empathy, and perspective-taking in resolving conflicts and the role of mediation and negotiation in facilitating constructive dialogue and problem-solving. Lastly, we will explore the role of leadership in modeling and promoting healthy conflict resolution behaviors, creating a culture where differences are seen as opportunities for growth and innovation rather than sources of division and discord.

5 Simple Techniques for Resolving Conflict

1. **Be an Active Listener**: Work to listen actively and attentively without interruptions. This involves focusing on fully understanding the speaker's perspective, demonstrating empathy through nonverbal cues, and asking clarifying questions to ensure comprehension. Active listening is crucial for finding common ground and resolving conflicts amicably. Resolving conflict involves participating in a dialogue, not delivering a monologue.
2. **Seek Compromise**: Find common ground and explore mutually acceptable solutions through compromise. This involves identifying shared interests and brainstorming solutions that address the needs and concerns of all parties involved. By focusing on common goals and being willing to make concessions, compromise can help resolve conflicts and promote cooperation.
3. **Use "I" Statements**: Express your feelings and concerns using "I" statements, which focus on personal experiences rather than attributing blame or making accusations. For example, instead of saying, "You always ignore my ideas," consider saying, "I feel frustrated when I perceive that my ideas are not being considered." "I" statements promote open communication and reduce defensiveness, making it easier to address conflicts constructively.
4. **Take a Break or a Pause**: If emotions are running high or communication has become unproductive, take a break from the conflict. This could involve temporarily stepping away from the situation to cool off and gain perspective before resuming the discussion, or pausing in the conversation if you are being interrupted. Taking a break allows individuals to regroup, refocus, and approach the conflict with a clearer mindset, to allow for more productive conversations and resolutions.
5. **Mediation**: Consider involving a mediator to facilitate communication and help reach a resolution. A mediator can provide an objective perspective, facilitate constructive dialogue, and help parties resolve conflict and find common ground.

5 Ways to Model Conflict Resolution as a Leader

1. **Remain Calm Under Pressure**: Demonstrate composure and poise during conflicts, avoid blaming and shaming, maintain a calm demeanor, and avoid reactive or defensive responses. By modeling emotional resilience and self-control, you set a positive tone and help create an environment where tensions can be diffused and conflicts can be resolved constructively.
2. **Seek Win-Win Solutions**: Encourage collaborative problem-solving by seeking win-win solutions that address the needs and interests of all parties involved. Instead of resorting to win-lose tactics or power struggles, demonstrate your commitment to finding mutually beneficial outcomes that preserve relationships and promote teamwork.
3. **Show Empathy and Understanding**: Offer empathy and understanding towards all parties involved in conflicts, acknowledging their perspectives, feelings, and concerns. By demonstrating empathy, you create a supportive and inclusive environment where individuals feel heard, valued, and respected, even when they disagree.
4. **Respect Boundaries and Confidentiality**: Respect confidentiality and boundaries when resolving conflicts, and refrain from sharing sensitive information or personal details without permission. Avoid disclosing information shared with you in confidentiality to prove your point. By modeling respect for privacy and confidentiality, you foster trust and create a safe space for individuals to address conflicts openly and honestly.
5. **Promote Constructive Communication**: Encourage open and constructive communication during conflicts, fostering an atmosphere where individuals feel comfortable expressing their viewpoints and concerns. By modeling effective communication techniques, such as using "I" statements (see previous page), staying focused on the issue, and avoiding personal attacks, you facilitate productive dialogue and help move conflicts toward resolution.

CHAPTER 9: BUILDING TRUST AND EMPOWERMENT AMONG EMPLOYEES

Trust is the currency of collaboration, enabling individuals and teams to work together towards common goals with confidence and mutual respect. In this chapter, we explore strategies for building trust and empowerment among employees, from fostering a culture of inclusion and belonging to providing opportunities for skill development and autonomy.

We will delve into the importance of authentic leadership, transparency, and consistency in earning and maintaining trust within organizations. Moreover, we will examine the role of empowerment in unlocking the full potential of individuals and teams, fostering creativity, innovation, and engagement. By prioritizing trust and empowerment, we create environments where individuals feel respected and motivated to contribute their best work.

I hope this section empowers you to take action and drive positive change within your organizations, transforming toxic workplaces into environments where individuals thrive and organizations flourish.

Fostering a Culture of Inclusion and Belonging:

At the heart of building trust and empowerment lies a culture of inclusion and belonging - where every individual feels valued, respected, and accepted for who they are. Organizations can foster this culture by promoting diversity, equity, inclusion, and accessibility (DEIA) initiatives, celebrating differences, and creating opportunities for all voices to be heard. By prioritizing inclusivity, organizations build trust among employees and empower individuals to bring their authentic selves to work.

Authentic Leadership:

Authentic leadership plays a pivotal role in establishing and upholding trust within organizations. Leaders who lead with authenticity, by being transparent, vulnerable, and true to themselves, inspire trust and confidence in their teams. By modeling integrity, honesty, and humility, leaders foster a culture of trust and empowerment. This type of leadership is beneficial for the organization and the leader's personal growth and development.

Transparency and Consistency:

Transparency and consistency are crucial elements of building trust in any relationship, personal or professional. Communicating openly, sharing information freely, and operating with integrity fosters trust among employees within a team or organization. Consistent behavior and decision-making reinforce trust, demonstrating that leaders are reliable and trustworthy. By prioritizing transparency and consistency, we create environments where trust flourishes, and individuals feel empowered to take risks, innovate, and collaborate.

Empowerment for Growth and Innovation:

Empowerment is the key to unlocking the full potential of individuals and teams. By providing employees with opportunities for skill development, autonomy, and decision-making authority, organizations foster a sense of ownership and accountability. Empowered employees are more engaged, creative, and motivated to contribute their ideas and solutions. By empowering individuals, organizations drive innovation, foster a culture of continuous learning, and create environments where employees have higher job satisfaction and they continuously thrive.

Taking Action for Positive Change:

As we wrap up our discussion on building trust and empowerment among employees, I urge you to "walk the talk." These principles have the power to transform workplaces, making them healthier and more productive. By prioritizing trust, authenticity, transparency, and empowerment, we create environments where individuals feel they belong and bring their "A Game" to work daily. I encourage you to take action and drive positive change to ensure that toxicity is not tolerated and is actively opposed.

5 Simple Techniques to Build Trust

1. **Consistency and Reliability**: Consistently deliver on your promises and commitments. Whether it's meeting deadlines, following through on tasks, or honoring agreements, demonstrating reliability builds trust over time. Be transparent about what you can and cannot do, and consistently strive to meet or exceed expectations.
2. **Open Communication**: Foster a culture of open communication where colleagues feel comfortable sharing their thoughts, concerns, and feedback. Encourage opportunities for dialogue by actively listening to others, providing constructive feedback, and being approachable and receptive to differing perspectives. Transparent communication helps build trust by promoting honesty, clarity, and mutual understanding.
3. **Demonstrate Competence**: Continuously strive to develop and improve your skills and knowledge in your role. By demonstrating competence and expertise in your role, you instill confidence in your abilities and earn the trust of your colleagues and leader. Share your expertise generously, mentor others, and seek opportunities to contribute to the success of your team and organization.
4. **Implement The Golden Rule**: Treat others as you wish to be treated, with empathy, kindness, and respect. Take the time to understand their perspectives, feelings, and needs, and demonstrate an understanding of their perspective by offering support and encouragement when needed. Respect diverse viewpoints, experiences, and backgrounds, and be an advocate or ally for others if their voices are being silenced.
5. **Encourage Vulnerability and Authenticity:** Create a safe space where colleagues feel comfortable being vulnerable and authentic. Encourage sharing personal experiences, challenges, and successes, fostering deeper connections and empathy across the team. By embracing vulnerability and authenticity, you model those qualities and encourage others to do the same, ultimately strengthening trust within the team.

Self-Reflective Questions for Section 3: Strategies for Resolution and Prevention

Let's take one last pause to reflect on the following questions to evaluate ways you can support the resolution and prevention of toxicity in your workplace:

- **How can I advocate for a culture of accountability and transparency within my team or organization?**
    - *How can I hold individuals accountable for their actions, encourage open communication, and advocate for clear policies and procedures?*

- **What steps can I take to foster a culture of respect and inclusivity among my colleagues?**
    - *How can I help create a culture of respect and inclusivity? What more can I do to respect diverse perspectives, speak up against discrimination or bias, and actively support initiatives that promote diversity and inclusion?*

- **How can I effectively address conflict and diffuse tension within my team or organization?**
    - *What are some strategies I could implement to address conflict constructively? How can I improve my active listening, empathetic communication, and mediation skills? How can I de-escalate tensions and promote healthy conflict resolution within my workplace?*

- **How can I support the well-being and mental health of my colleagues?**
    - *How can I better offer a listening ear, provide emotional support, and encourage self-care practices with my colleagues?*

- **How can I advocate for change and challenge toxic organizational norms or behaviors?**
    - *How can I speak up against inappropriate conduct, support initiatives for cultural change, and actively participate in efforts to promote a healthier workplace culture?*

Conclusion

Moving Towards Healthier Workplaces

As we draw to a close on our journey through the intricacies of toxic workplaces, I hope you emerge not only armed with knowledge but also with a renewed sense of purpose and enthusiasm to make your workplace more collaborative, supportive, and fun. The path to healthier workplaces is not a destination but a continuous journey of growth, adaptation, and transformation. I hope you will reflect on the importance of continuous evaluation and adaptation, the necessity of creating long-term solutions for sustainable change, and the imperative of empowering individuals and organizations to thrive beyond toxicity.

The Importance of Continuous Evaluation and Adaptation

Toxicity, like a stubborn weed, has a knack for resurfacing in unexpected ways. Thus, continuous evaluation and adaptation are essential to maintaining a healthy organizational environment. Just as a gardener tends to their garden, we must cultivate a culture of vigilance, where issues are identified early, and corrective action is taken swiftly.

Moreover, we must be willing to adapt our approaches and strategies in response to changing circumstances and emerging challenges. What worked yesterday may not work tomorrow; therefore, we must remain flexible and open-minded, embracing innovation and experimentation as we strive to create workplaces where individuals truly enjoy coming to work each day.

Creating Long-Term Solutions for Sustainable Change

While quick fixes may offer temporary relief, true transformation requires a commitment to long-term solutions. Band-Aid solutions may address symptoms, but they do little to address the underlying causes of toxicity. To create lasting change, we must be willing to tackle root causes head-on, challenging entrenched norms, behaviors, and structures that perpetuate toxicity.

This requires courage, perseverance, and a willingness to confront uncomfortable truths. It may involve reevaluating longstanding practices, reimagining organizational structures, and cultivating new norms and values. It is a journey with many obstacles, but the reward - a healthier, more vibrant workplace - is well worth the effort.

Empowering Individuals and Organizations to Thrive Beyond Toxicity

Ultimately, the key to building healthier workplaces lies in empowerment — empowering individuals to speak up, take action, and champion positive change and empowering organizations to embrace a culture of transparency, accountability, and continuous improvement.

This empowerment begins with education and awareness, equipping individuals with the knowledge and tools to recognize and address toxicity in all its forms. It extends to fostering a culture of psychological safety, where individuals feel empowered to speak their minds, take risks, and challenge the status quo without fear of reprisal.

It culminates in creating environments where individuals are valued, respected, and empowered to thrive. It is a vision worth striving for - a vision of workplaces where toxicity has no place to hide, and where individuals and organizations can prosper and reach their highest potential.

As we bid farewell to the pages of this book, let us carry forward the lessons learned and the insights gained and commit ourselves to building healthier, more inclusive workplaces where toxicity is but a distant memory. Along your journey, refer back to this book as needed, if things become challenging, but together, we can create a brighter, more promising future for all.

Be the leader you've always needed. Create the workplace you've always wanted.

CONCLUSION: JUST THE BEGINNING

As we conclude our journey through the intricacies of toxic workplaces, it's important to recognize that this exploration is just the beginning of a broader conversation about fostering healthier, more supportive professional environments. I trust "Decoding Toxic Workplaces" has provided valuable insights into identifying, understanding, and addressing toxic dynamics within organizations. We've learned about the damaging impact of toxic leadership, dysfunctional team behaviors, and the importance of cultivating a culture of respect and accountability.

However, our work doesn't stop here. I'm excited to announce my next book, "The Anti-Manager's Playbook: How NOT to Lead Like a B*tch or a Buffoon," which will delve deeper into the critical role of effective leadership in shaping workplace culture. Drawing from my experiences and research, this upcoming book will offer practical strategies and anecdotes that humorously explore the pitfalls of ineffective management for new and seasoned leaders.

As we move forward, let's remember the key lessons from "Decoding Toxic Workplaces": the significance of open communication, the necessity of setting healthy boundaries, and the power of collective action in combating toxicity. Stay tuned for "The Anti-Manager's Playbook," where we'll continue to navigate the complexities of organizational dynamics and uncover the secrets to fostering thriving, respectful workplaces for all. Together, let's redefine what it means to lead with integrity and empathy.

~ *Jessica Jones*

Jessica Jones
Info@thecodegroup.org
www.thecodegroup.org

Printed in Great Britain
by Amazon